Elephant Imprints
PO BOX 2912
Rowville 3178
Victoria, Australia
www.elephantimprints.com

Published by Elephant Imprints in 2021

Text © Nicole Connellan, 2021
Illustrations © Selina Chuo, 2021

All rights reserved. No part of this publication may be reproduced or transmitted in any form or by any means, electronic or mechanical, including photocopying, recording, or by any information storage and retrieval system or otherwise, without the prior written permission of the publisher, unless specifically permitted under the Australian Copyright Act: 1968 as amended.

National Library of Australia
Cataloguing-in-Publication entry
Creator: Connellan, Nicole, author.
Title: The Story of a Movement : Part Two / Nicole Connellan ; Selina Chuo
ISBN: 978-0-6488599-2-5 (paperback)
ISBN: 978-0-6488599-3-2 (hardback)
Target Audience: For children
Other Creators/Contributors: Chuo, Selina, illustrator.

Typeset in ABeeZee.

www.thestoryof2020.com

The Story of a MOVEMENT

NICOLE CONNELLAN & SELINA CHUO

The story of 2020
continued with a movement.
Not everyone was treated well,
so we called for big improvements.

We all have unique features:
our eyes, skin and hair.
Though we may have different stories,
there's a future we will all share.

Being different isn't a problem.
Every race is unique and strong.
The problems start when some believe
you must look alike to belong.

More bad news, different stories.
More sad videos, different phones.
How badly could others be treated
just for having different skin tones?

Numbness,

anger,

sadness,

these were the expressed reactions.

These things continued happening
      because of decades of inaction.

Support and generosity were poured out day to day.

But then the protests and the strikes
made many people livid.
How much interruption would it take
for justice to be considered?

Not everyone agreed
with the fires or the marches.
Could it demand attention
from those able to lay charges?

We may have felt uncomfortable seeing all these things unfold.
Yet occasions arose for us to discuss the values we uphold.

Racism wasn't the only issue receiving lots of mentions. The treatment of others, in every way, also got attention.

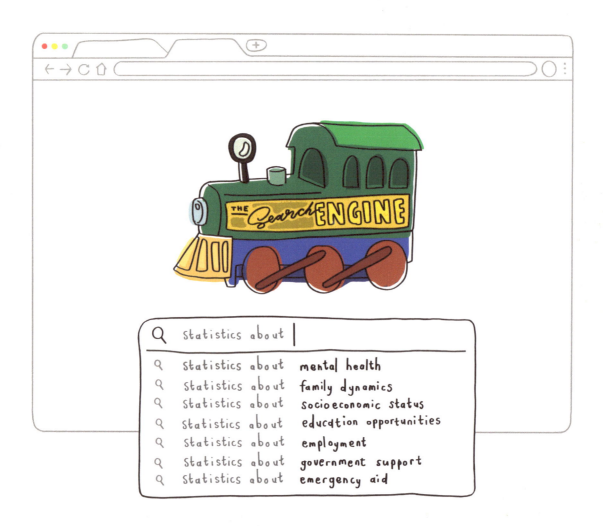

There's injustice all around us

that is sad and very serious.

And if nobody talks about it,

these issues stay mysterious.

Each of us has influence: by example and in choice.
Do your words and actions match the passion in your voice?

Do you have empathy? Love with action?
And take the time to listen?
Is being right more about showing kindness without condition?

We need these conversations from the ground up to the top.

What changes can we make
so that discrimination stops?

Mistakes are part of learning.
We all make a handful or three.
As we become a caring community,
imperfection is guaranteed.

We think we know, but really we don't.
It's always better to ask.

If something affects other people,
involve them in the task.

We are all valuable, in and out.
All skin will bleed the same.
And when we care to heal all wounds,
the world is better framed.

What does that mean?

Adults (parents, grandparents, teachers, trusted adults) are encouraged to read these next pages with children and to give room for questions, discussions and sharing of personal experiences.

This story is for children, but it wasn't written for children to read alone. It's unlikely children will understand all of the details or concepts, even with the illustrations and rhyme. And while it isn't an 'easy read', hopefully you decide it's a very worthwhile one. As adults, we try to introduce our children to what we consider are important concepts from an early age. Valuing all people is one of those fundamental concepts.

This story might be an introduction to racism, or a prompt to help articulate what children have observed but haven't had explained. It does not need to be thoroughly discussed in a single sitting. Be mindful of the sensitivity and maturity of the children reading it with you.

And always try to end the conversation with hope.

RACISM
What is it?

Racism is thinking less of others because of where they are from, their culture or the colour of their skin.

Racism can take many forms:

- always joking about and not taking some people seriously
- not wanting to be near them
- not choosing them in opportunities
- thinking they are not as important, smart or valuable as others
- blaming them for bad things happening
- being afraid of them and assuming they are the enemy
- wanting them to fail and not helping them
- telling them to be more 'normal' and to tone down their culture (assimilate)
- not respecting the significance given to traditions and events of different cultures

It can be as bad as hating others without knowing them, and as simple as thinking you know all about someone when you don't. It often involves people trying to control what others can do simply because of how they look or where they are from.

"*We're so sorry you experienced racism*"

我们很想念您呢。

Because COVID-19 was first identified in China, Chinese people all around the world have experienced hate crimes (attacks fuelled by racism). But, blaming someone who looks Chinese for the COVID-19 virus is like being angry at every dog owner because cats can get fleas. It makes no sense and it doesn't make anything better.

"*A greater threat was exposed*"

Haven't felt safe anywhere.

Which is more dangerous? A highly contagious virus? Or racism? Both have led to too many deaths. More dangerous than a virus that doesn't discriminate is knowing so many people believe it is okay to hurt others.

There is no vaccine for hate, and it can also be contagious.

"More bad news, different stories"

Tragic stories were often in the news about people who were treated as though their lives weren't important because of the colour of their skin. For many people, these stories showed the same racism that had been experienced many times, just affecting different families.

"More sad videos, different phones"

People of colour started using their phones to film the moments they experienced racist treatment. This was because video footage couldn't be disregarded or ignored as easily as their reported experience, especially when it was shared.

Many of these videos shared over social media exposed the different ways community members responded to racism. It also spread awareness about how disruptive and damaging racism is. And sometimes, the videos meant people could be held accountable for their actions.

"These things continued happening because of decades of inaction"

Laws are the rules we live by. They are meant to make things fair, but they haven't been fair for everyone.

If the laws haven't been fair, they need to change so all people can be safe.

But the only way they will change is if a lot of people openly agree it should change.

If you have never felt that things have been unfair for you, you are privileged.

Many systems are built on laws that allow for unfair treatment of others. This can happen in education, healthcare, workplaces, the justice system, housing, support services, and at every single life opportunity. But all systems work because people make it work, so the attitudes of leaders and communities need to change too.

"These things continued happening because of decades of inaction" means that not enough changed over many, many years. Countless people were hurt because the law didn't protect them, blamed them for things that they didn't do, and sometimes even defended offenders more than those who were hurt. This made many people feel unsafe, sad and angry.

For a country to decide that laws need changing, we all need to understand when things are not working. If more people are aware when things are unfair, and care about the people affected, then the big community response can power momentum for law makers to change laws.

"How much interruption would it take for justice to be considered?"

"Not everyone agreed with the fires or the marches.

Could it demand attention from those able to lay charges?"

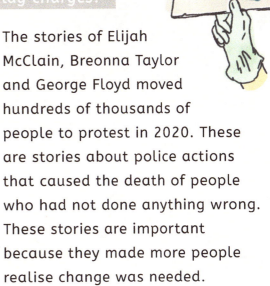

There were strikes and protests by many people, but often the spotlight was on sportspeople who chose not to play as a stand against violence. Many of these sportspeople were black. Choosing not to play prompted many people to talk about why their favourite sport wasn't on, and it started conversations (and arguments) about what was more important.

The stories of Elijah McClain, Breonna Taylor and George Floyd moved hundreds of thousands of people to protest in 2020. These are stories about police actions that caused the death of people who had not done anything wrong. These stories are important because they made more people realise change was needed.

"There's injustice all around us that is sad and very serious. And if nobody talks about it, these issues stay mysterious"

In every part of our world, at every age and for every opportunity, things will probably be unfair for somebody. However, it isn't obvious until you've experienced it personally. If people don't advocate for those who are not treated fairly, then nothing will change. This means listening to other people who need help, asking them what they need, and making sure they are heard by somebody who can help.

"Is being right more about showing kindness without condition?"

Disagreements happen. It's natural, normal and healthy. But fighting over who is right or wrong can be upsetting, especially when one or both sides of the conversation get heated. Being 'right' in a disagreement doesn't mean it is right to make others feel bad for not agreeing. Opinions are not more important than people. Sometimes the best thing to do is to agree to disagree.

Kindness should be unconditional. Being kind to only the people that

you like and who agree with you is favouritism. And racism is built on favouritism.

We shouldn't treat others a certain way because we decide they 'deserve it'. We should treat everyone with the same kindness and respect we would like to be treated with. Remember, you may not feel comfortable with everyone, but you can still be respectful to everyone.

"What changes can we make so that discrimination stops?"

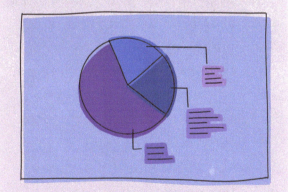

How can we make sure nobody is treated unfairly because of their culture, age, gender or ability?

"As we become a caring community, imperfection is guaranteed"

Our leaders won't make perfect decisions every time or completely agree on outcomes. However, communities can work together to highlight issues and problem solve.

This hand with only 3 fingers wasn't a mistake. Most people have 5 fingers on each hand, but not everybody does. This person has a limb difference (called symbrachydactyly), but it doesn't stop them from calling for change. Often people with a disability (and their families) fight the hardest for everyone to be treated fairly, because they know how it feels to be treated badly.

"We are all valuable, in and out. All skin will bleed the same."

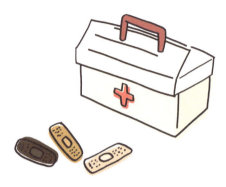

The human body is incredible. Our skin is the largest organ and most protective part of our body. We should all appreciate that, yet this organ that protects us can also be the thing that makes us look different. A pigment called melanin gives our hair, skin and eyes their colour.

There's nothing wrong with noticing physical differences. But we should definitely focus more on the quality of people's character.

"And when we care to heal all wounds..."

Did you know it took almost 100 years for adhesive bandages to come in a range of skin tones? It took a really long time for this industry to recognise "flesh coloured" wasn't just pale pink. That might not seem like a big deal, but when diversity is not recognised, then every little thing adds up to give small but frequent messages that some people don't need to be considered.

What can kids do?

Observe:

Look around you. Do you see different cultures in your class, your school, your community, in leadership? How about in your favourite TV shows and movies? What about in ads or posters? What cultural food choices are available at your school canteen or in your local food court? Are the people in your community reflected in the choices provided? If you don't notice diversity, you might not notice racism.

Notice the words and body language used when talking about others. What tone of voice is used? Is another person or culture described positively, negatively or neutrally? If you notice people are treated differently when they do the same thing, call attention to it.

Care:

When we care about others, we care when things go well or wrong for them. If you notice people not being treated well or if something doesn't seem right, tell a trusted adult about it. Together, you can see if there's anything you can do about it. And if you see someone who needs help and you can give it, then do. It might be as simple as a smile.

Ask:

See colour everywhere, value everyone and ask questions when you don't see diversity.

Ask your parents or other trusted adults if they've ever been treated unfairly. Hearing somebody else's story can help you learn about forgiveness, maturity and what to look out for. If you're not sure what you saw or heard was racism— maybe it was someone just being grumpy— tell a trusted adult what happened and talk about it.

Learn:

Ask your parents to help you find good, age appropriate books or an interesting documentary/series (that you'll both like) that has main characters from different cultures and countries. It doesn't matter if they're made up or based on true stories. Both are usually well researched. When you see and hear different stories, you learn about different lives and that expands your understanding of humanity.

Accept differences:

If you have friends who do things really differently, don't say "That's weird!" Because what you're really saying is "I am and my ways are **normal**".

Anyone who is different from you is not weird or wrong. Differences should be safe to talk about, especially with friends and family. Instead of labelling something unfamiliar as "weird" or "ridiculous", try saying "I've never heard that before, can you tell me about it?" Then listen to learn about somebody else's story. Accepting we are not experts in other people's lives is important.

If someone you don't know makes you feel uncomfortable because they look different, talk about it with a trusted adult. Did that person walk differently, have an unusual expression, sound, look or act in a way that made you scared or unsure? Be aware of what makes you uncomfortable and talk to a trusted adult about whether this is reasonable or not. Be mindful that calling someone else suspicious or dangerous is usually more harmful for the other person.

Have good conversations:

It matters what and how we say things.

Try to state your point calmly and neutrally. Being emotional is not wrong, but staying calm helps you to think clearly. When we make mistakes (by accident or on purpose), we all prefer to be told about it calmly rather than being screamed at.

Try not to accuse anyone of being "racist". We want to call out the wrong perspectives and inconsistent behaviour, not target people as the enemy. Accusing somebody of racism gives little room for talking about what happened and learning from it, on both sides.

It's also important to hear all sides of the story. It's hard to build trust if people are quicker to accuse than to try work out a solution. And it's unlikely people will apologise for their actions if they don't understand how they upset you. Caring about EVERYBODY means caring about the person whose actions may have seemed racist. It's not easy caring about everybody, but that is what we try to do.

Remember similarities:

Think about the person who is the most unlike you. Are they in your family, in your school or at your sports club? Is it hard to get along with them? Sometimes it helps to find out what you have in common with very different people. It doesn't mean you have to be best friends. It just means you take the time to listen to someone different. And that should be something everyone does more often.

Remember,
everyone has a family.
Everyone is valuable.
Just like you.

Everyone has hopes,
dreams, fears and worries.
Just like you.

Everyone makes mistakes.
Everyone does and says
silly things sometimes.
Just like you.

And everyone appreciates
being listened to and cared
about. Just like you.

Acknowledgements:

Thank you Jenny Flynn (Composed Writing) for editing both Part One and Part Two.

Thank you Ken Ji, for permission to use your photos as references for illustrations.

Thank you to Sofia Cabral, May Loh, Daniel Connellan and Tash Haynes for your time in reviewing and feedback.

Family and friends, thank you for your support and encouragement always.

Finally, the deepest appreciation to God for the opportunity and inspiration to create and share to the best of our abilities.

CPSIA information can be obtained
at www.ICGtesting.com
Printed in the USA
BVHW021101090621
609090BV00002B/27